THE **7** CONTINENTS

A
S
I
A

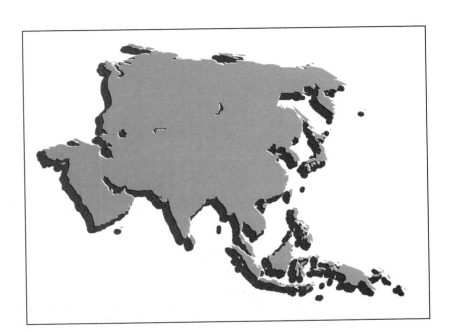

APRIL PULLEY SAYRE

TWENTY-FIRST CENTURY BOOKS
BROOKFIELD, CONNECTICUT

For my wonderful editor, Virginia A. Koeth, who has climbed mountains of text, bridged conceptual gaps, navigated shifting continents, waded through baffling biomes, and restored my spirits, time and time again.

—A.P.S.

Published by Twenty-First Century Books
A Division of The Millbrook Press, Inc.
2 Old New Milford Road
Brookfield, Connecticut 06804

Text copyright © 1999 by April Pulley Sayre
Maps by Joe LeMonnier
All rights reserved.

Library of Congress Cataloging-in-Publication Data
Sayre, April Pulley.
Asia / April Pulley Sayre.
p. cm. — (The seven continents)
Includes bibliographical references and index.
Summary: Describes the landscapes, geology, weather, oceans, coastlines,
air, soil, plants, animals, and people of the continent of Asia.

ISBN 0-7613-1368-0 (lib.bdg.)
1. Asia—Juvenile literature. [1. Asia.] I. Title.
II. Series: Sayre, April Pulley. 7 continents.
DS5.S29 1999
50—dc21   98-48906
                                                                      CIP
                                                                      AC

Printed in the United States of America
1 3 5 4 2

Photo Credits

Cover photograph courtesy of © Lynn M. Stone

Photographs courtesy of Naomi Duguid/Asia Access: pp. 8, 42; Photo Researchers: p. 11 (© Gerhardt Liebmann); The National Audubon Society Collection/Photo Researchers: pp. 14 (© Alvin E. Staffan), 50 (© Michael Tweedie); © Sovfoto/Eastfoto: pp. 16, 19, 28, 29, 36, 39; Peter Arnold, Inc.: pp. 17 (© Fred Bruemmer), 26 (© Fritz Polking), 31 (© John Wark), 43 (© Fateh Singh Rathore), 45 (© John Paul Kay); NGS Image Collection: pp. 22 (© Dr. Cynthia M. Beall and Melvyn C. Goldstein), 32 (© Michael Nichols); © Liaison Agency, Inc.: pp. 33 (Mustafa Cetinkaya), 47 (Edwin Tuyay)

CONTENTS

CONTINENTS: WHERE WE STAND

The ground you stand on may seem solid and stable, but it's really moving all the time. How is that possible? Because all of the earth's continents, islands, oceans, and people ride on tectonic plates. These plates, which are huge slabs of the earth's crust, float on top of hot, melted rock below. One plate may carry a whole continent and a piece of an ocean. Another may carry only a few islands and some ocean. The plates shift, slide, and even bump together slowly as the molten rock below them flows.

Plate edges are where the action is, geologically speaking. That's where volcanoes erupt and earthquakes shake the land. Tectonic plates collide, gradually crumpling continents into folds that become mountains. Dry land, or ocean floor, can be made at these plate edges. Melted rock, spurting out of volcanoes or oozing out of cracks between plates, cools and solidifies. Dry land, or ocean floor, can also be destroyed here, as the edge of one tectonic plate slips underneath another. The moving, grinding plates create tremendous pressure and heat, which melts the rock, turning it into semisolid material.

Continents, the world's largest landmasses, the rock rafts where we live, ride on this shifting puzzle of tectonic plates. These continents are made of material that floated to the surface when much of the earth was hot and liquid long ago. The floating material then cooled and became solid. Two hundred and fifty million years ago there was only one continent, the supercontinent Pangaea, surrounded by one ocean, Panthalassa. But since then, the tectonic plates have moved, breaking apart the continents and rearranging them. Today there are seven continents: North America, South America, Europe, Asia, Africa, Australia, and Antarctica.

250 Million Years Ago

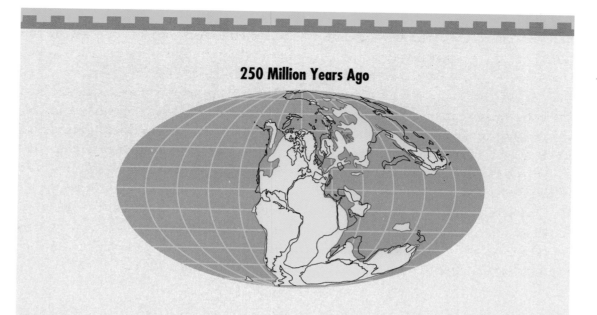

Two hundred and fifty million years ago there was only one continent and one ocean, as shown above. (Rough shapes the continents would eventually take are outlined in black.) The view below shows where the seven continents are today. These positions will continue to change slowly as tectonic plates shift.

Present Day

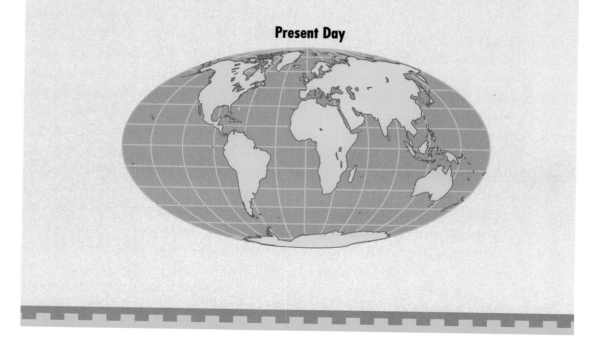

Each continent has its own unique character and conditions, shaped by its history and position on the earth. Europe, which is connected to Asia, has lots of coastline and moist, ocean air. Australia, meanwhile, is influenced by its neighbor, Antarctica, which sends cool currents northward to its shores. North America and South America were once separated, but are now connected by Panama. Over the years, animals, from ancient camels to armadillos, have traveled the bridge in between these two continents.

A continent's landscape, geology, weather, and natural communities affect almost every human action taken on that continent, from planting a seed to waging a war. Rivers become the borders of countries. Soil determines what we can grow. Weather and climate affect our cultures—what we feel, how we dress, even how we celebrate.

Understanding continents can give us a deeper knowledge of the earth—its plants, animals, and people. It can help us see behind news headlines to appreciate the forces that shape world events. Such knowledge can be helpful, especially in a world that's constantly changing and shifting, down to the very earth beneath our feet.

A vast continent, Asia is a study in contrasts. Here the Takla Makan Desert fills the foreground, while the background is formed by the snowcapped peaks of the Pamir Mountains.

ONE

ASIA: THE BIGGEST OF ALL

The largest continent on earth stretches from the icy Arctic to the steamy tropics. It's bigger than North and South America, combined. East to west, Asia is so wide that it covers eleven time zones. When it is 3:00 P.M. in Israel, on the other side of the continent, in Japan, it is 1:00 A.M. and the next day is beginning!

Asia contains many of the world's largest deserts, forests, and plateaus. It has towering mountains, as well. The sixty highest mountains in the world are located in Asia, mostly in Nepal, China, India, Pakistan, and Bhutan. Earth's highest point, Mount Everest, is located in the Himalayas, an Asian mountain range, which is rising higher, year by year.

Asia has big animals and plants, too. (Although Africa has the biggest land animals of all.) Asian elephants weigh in at a maximum of 12,000 pounds (5.4 metric tons.) The world's biggest bats, the flying foxes of Southeast Asia, have a wingspan of as much as 5 feet (1.5 meters). Indonesia also has monitor lizards, which can be 10 feet (3 meters) long and weigh 300 pounds (136 kilograms)! Of course, Asia's natural wonders aren't impressive just because they are big or tall or vast. Southeast Asia's tropical rain forests contain an incredible biodiversity—a variety of species from beetles to butterflies to birds. The Asian tundra, taiga, grasslands, deserts, and steppes are home to reindeer, moose, wild sheep, wild cattle, and wild goats. No one knows how many Asian animals have yet to be discovered, named, and studied by scientists. Biologists recently found two new deer species living in the mountains of Vietnam!

Asia, the largest of all the continents, also has the largest number of people. Yet because much of Asia is dry desert or high mountain or cold, frozen tundra, Asia's people tend to be crowded in the warm, wet, low-lying regions along southern rivers and coastlines. These areas are attractive because riversides are fertilized by seasonal floods that deposit rich soil, which is good for agriculture. Islands and coastlines give the Asian people access to fishing, shipping, and other aquatic resources.

ASIA'S CONTINENTAL NEIGHBORS

Where does Asia end and Europe begin? It depends on who you ask. In the west, Asia is physically joined to Europe. Many geographers consider Europe a peninsula of Asia. They call the combination of the two, Eurasia. Other geographers consider Europe separate from Asia, primarily because of differences between Asian and European cultures.

NEWSWORTHY WORDS

Lots of news about Asia never mentions the word Asia. Instead, reporters talk about the Middle East, or Siberia, or the Pacific Rim. What they are describing are very general Asian regions, or groups of Asian countries. Look at a map and memorize the regional terms below, and you'll have a head start on understanding Asian news.

- Indian Subcontinent—the part of India, south of the Himalayas, that juts out into the Indian Ocean. India, Bangladesh, and Pakistan are located on the Indian Subcontinent.
- Southeast Asia—a general term for countries in the southeast of the continent, usually including Myanmar (Burma), Thailand, Malaysia, Laos, Cambodia, Vietnam, Indonesia, Singapore, and the Philippines.
- The Middle East—the countries of southwest Asia, and northeast Africa. Middle Eastern countries in Asia include: Cyprus, Israel, Jordan, Lebanon, Syria, Turkey, Bahrain, Iran, Iraq, Kuwait, Oman, Qatar, Saudi Arabia, United Arab Emirates, and Yemen.
- The Orient, or the East—a very general term for countries in Asia.
- The Far East—eastern and southeastern Asia, usually the countries of: Myanmar, Cambodia, China, Indonesia, Japan, North Korea, South Korea, Laos, Malaysia, the Philippines, Taiwan, and Vietnam. Sometimes also refers to Mongolia and eastern Russia.
- Siberia—a vast, cold, windswept, sparsely populated region located mostly in Russia. Siberia stretches from the Ural Mountains in the west to the Pacific Ocean on the east.
- Arabian Peninsula—the peninsula in southwest Asia occupied by Saudi Arabia, Oman, Qatar, United Arab Emirates, and Yemen.

The Ural Mountains that cut southward through Russia form much of the accepted border between Europe and Asia. From the Urals, the boundary runs down to the north shore of the Caspian Sea, then westward along the crest of the Caucasus Mountains. Asia's western border then skirts the north shore of the Black Sea and crosses the Bosporus Strait, dividing Turkey where the Black Sea connects to the Aegean Sea. Because of this somewhat awkward border, five countries are shared by Asia and Europe: Russia, Turkey, Kazakhstan, Georgia, and Azerbaijan. Egypt is shared by Asia and Africa.

OTHER CONTINENTAL NEIGHBORS

Asia wraps around the earth, 4,000 miles (6,440 kilometers) from north to south and 6,000 miles (9,650 kilometers) east to west. It stretches so far and wide that its edges are close to other continents. Asia's southernmost islands, in the country of Indonesia, are not far from Australia. Africa, too, is a close neighbor. People could once walk from Asia to Africa on dry land. But then, in the 1860s, the Suez Canal was built, to carry ship traffic from the Mediterranean Sea to the Red Sea. Once the 101-mile (163-kilometer) Suez Canal was dug and filled with water, it separated the surfaces of the two continents. (It divided a country, too. Most of Egypt is located in Africa, but the eastern portion, cut off by the Suez Canal, is located in Asia.)

Ships of all sizes can be found sailing in the Suez Canal. Built in the 1860s, the canal separates Asia from Africa.

Asia and North America have been physically joined, at times. During the last ice age, between 11,000 and 40,000 years ago, people and caribou could walk from Asia to North America on dry land. During ice ages, when more of earth's water is frozen in glaciers and ice caps, sea levels tend to be lower. So back then, people could cross the Bering Land Bridge, a section of land that connects what is now eastern Russia and western Alaska. No one can walk overland between these two continents anymore, because since the last ice age, the sea level has risen and covered up the Bering Land Bridge. However, the easternmost islands of Russia still lie only 3 miles (4.8 kilometers) from the islands of Alaska.

WORLD RECORDS HELD BY ASIA

- Largest continent: 17,139,445 square miles (44,391,162 square kilometers). Asia makes up about 30 percent of the earth's land area.
- Largest lake: Caspian Sea, 143,205 square miles (371,000 square kilometers)
- Highest mountain range: Himalayas, with the most peaks over 20,000 feet (6,000 meters)
- Highest point: Mount Everest, China/Nepal, 29,028 feet (8,848 meters)
- Second largest desert: Gobi, 500,000 square miles (1,295,000 square kilometers)
- Deepest lake: Lake Baikal, Russia, 5,715 feet (1,742 meters) deep
- Second and third largest islands: New Guinea, 342,000 square miles (885,780 square kilometers); Borneo, 290,320 square miles (751,929 square kilometers)
- Fourth longest river: Chang Jiang (Yangtze), China, 3,720 miles (5,989 kilometers)
- Largest country by area: Russia, 6,592,812 square miles (17,075,383 square kilometers)

STATISTICS AND RECORDS FOR THE CONTINENT OF ASIA

- Area: 17,139,445 square miles (44,391,162 square kilometers)—about 30 percent of the world's land
- Population: 3,460,000,000
- Lowest point: Dead Sea, Israel/Jordan, 1,292 feet (394 meters) below sea level
- Lowest recorded temperature: Verkhoyansk, Russia, –90°F (–68°C)
- Highest recorded temperature: Tirat Tsvi, Israel, 129°F (54°C)

T W O

COLD SPACES AND HIGH PLACES

Cold, windy, icy places are plentiful in Asia. You only have to travel north or climb a tall mountain to find them. In northern Russia, polar bears and arctic foxes leap from iceberg to iceberg. Walruses and seabirds crowd along shorelines to raise their young. This land is polar desert, with no trees, tall grasses, or shrubs. Most animals that live here find their food in the ocean. Farther south, but still cold in climate, arctic tundra and taiga have a wider variety of plants and animals.

ARCTIC TUNDRA

Just south of the polar desert is the arctic tundra, a treeless land where reindeer roam and snowy owls hunt. Like polar desert, arctic tundra is chilly and often windy. Air temperatures can drop to −58°F (−50°C) in winter. But in summer, air temperatures may rise above freezing. This slight warming allows the top few inches of ground to thaw, providing liquid water plants need. Tundra plants send shallow roots into this layer. Below the thawed soil is permafrost, permanently frozen ground.

Tundra plants seem to hug the ground. Being low growing keeps their leaves and branches under winter snow, protected from drying winds. Dwarf willow, dwarf birch, and dwarf juniper spread along the ground. Small arctic poppies and arctic pinks bloom in spring and summer, carpeting the tundra with color.

WATCH FOR BIRDS!

Look out for birds' nests if you walk on the tundra in summer. Many birds migrate to the treeless tundra, where they nest on the ground. Arctic terns make the longest trip, all

13

Long-distance champions, arctic terns migrate from Antarctica to the Arctic each year. Terns can be found nesting in tundra regions during summer.

the way from Antarctica to the Arctic to raise their young. Red-breasted geese, white-fronted geese, bean geese, king eiders, Siberian cranes, and Ross's gulls also nest on the tundra. Geese often nest near peregrine falcon nests, even though the falcons have a taste for other birds. The falcons, however, do not hunt near their nests. So the geese remain safe, at least while they are raising their young.

MUCK, MOSQUITOES, AND MAMMALS

Even though tundra receives only 8 to 10 inches (20 to 25 centimeters) of rain per year, the ground can be lumpy, soggy, and wet in summer. Plants form low growing mats and mounds. Water cannot drain through the permafrost, so it puddles on top, instead. The puddles, in summer, are a breeding ground for midges, gnats, and mosquitoes. These insects are an important food source for birds. But that's not much comfort to the people and reindeer trying to escape the thick clouds of biting bugs.

Reindeer, which are known as caribou in North America, often walk out onto snow-covered ground just to get away from biting flies. Reindeer spend the summer eating grasses and other plants on the tundra. In fall they migrate south to the taiga where they feed on lichens, flaky plantlike mats that grow on the ground, on rocks, and on trees. Lichens are a symbiotic partnership of fungi and algae. The algae live inside a fungus's tissues and carry out photosynthesis, providing the fungus with food. The algae, in return, is protected by the structure of the fungus, which also gathers the water and nutrients the algae need.

TAIGA: THE SPRUCE-MOOSE FOREST

Home to moose and great gray owls, the taiga is a place of tall trees, lichen-covered branches, and mossy ground. This forest, called northern coniferous forest, stretches in a broad belt across Russia. It's one of the largest forests in the world. At Verkhoyansk, Russia, temperatures have dipped down to –90°F (–68°C) in winter. But temperatures are usually around 66°F (19°C) in summer, although they can reach much higher. In some parts of Russia, the taiga is snowy. In other parts, it is fairly dry.

The forest is made up of towering trees such as Norway spruce, Siberian spruce, Siberian fir, and Siberian larch. They all have narrow leaves called needles and form cones, which contain seeds. Most of these trees are evergreen, which means they keep their leaves year round, only shedding a few at a time. Larch trees, however, are deciduous. They drop their leaves in fall. Birch trees, which have broad, deciduous leaves, grow in the taiga, too. But broad-leafed, deciduous trees such as birch are much more common south of the taiga, in the temperate deciduous forests of Asia.

SEEDY CHARACTERS AND MORE

In Siberian forests, red squirrels are only one of many species that eat seeds. Birds called crossbills use their crossed bills to pry open tree cones to get to the seeds. Another bird species, the nutcracker, grabs cones and smashes them against rocks to get out the seeds. Like a squirrel, the nutcracker also stashes seeds in cracks in trees. It will eat these caches—stored supplies—later, when food is scarce. But some uneaten seeds may sprout and grow.

DEEP AND ANCIENT: LAKE BAIKAL

Just north of Mongolia, in the Russian taiga, lies the world's oldest, deepest lake: Lake Baikal. Situated in a rift, a tremendous crack between tectonic plates, Baikal is more than 1 mile (1.6 kilometers) deep and holds one fifth of the fresh water on earth. Scientists believe the lake has existed for perhaps 25 million years, much longer than other lakes. (North America's Lake Superior, for instance, has only been around for 10,000 years or so.)

In winter the surface of Lake Baikal freezes so thick that trucks can drive across it. People drill holes in the ice and drop lines through to catch fish. Baikal seals also catch fish in the lake. These seals are one of almost 1,500 animal and plant species endemic to Lake Baikal, meaning they live nowhere else.

Lake Baikal is a source of wonder, national pride, and symbolic importance in Russia. In 1957, when the government revealed plans to build a paper mill at the lake's edge, people all around the lake protested. Even so, the paper mill was built. Today it emits air pollution and pumps waste into the lake. Despite the paper mill, some progress

Lake Baikal is a source of pride to the people who live along its shores.
Baikal is the oldest, deepest lake in the world.

in protecting Lake Baikal is being made. Environmentalists are pushing for better pollution controls. In 1987 the government abolished logging near the lake. Lakeside trees are important because their roots hold the soil in place, preventing dirt from being washed into the lake by heavy rains. Elementary-school children are getting involved, too. Many that live on the lake shores test the water for pollutants. The people of Russia cherish Lake Baikal and continue working to protect it.

HOW MANY, AND WHERE

Compared to warmer, wetter biomes such as tropical rain forest, polar desert, tundra, and taiga have relatively low biodiversity. Interestingly, many animal species in these regions are circumpolar, meaning they occur all around a pole, in this case the North Pole. Great gray owls, brown bears, polar bears, arctic foxes, wolverines, moose, and goshawks are only a few of the animals that inhabit not only the tundra and taiga of Asia but also of North America. The northern parts of these continents are very close together. During ice ages, when sea levels are low, or during cold winters when the ocean is iced over, birds and mammals can swim, fly, and walk in between these continents.

HIGH PLACES: MOUNTAINS

If you want to learn mountain climbing, don't start on Mount Everest. The summit of Mount Everest is the highest point on earth, towering 29,028 feet (8,848 meters) above sea level. At this dizzying height, winds gust to 150 miles (242 kilometers) per hour and windchills can be a flesh-freezing –97°F (–72°C). Glaciers—huge, slowly sliding masses of ice—drape the mountainsides. The percentage of oxygen in the air is so low that lack of oxygen makes many climbers dizzy and confused. Some suffer lung damage or brain

Ice that has been polished by the wind reflects the image of a polar bear, a circumpolar species.

damage, or even die. To avoid these problems, most hikers carry bottles of oxygen and breathe it through small masks, in order to climb the highest parts of Everest. Asia's tall mountains may be awe inspiring and beautiful, but their environmental conditions are harsh for people, animals, and plants.

IT'S NO LONGER LONELY AT THE TOP

The summit of Mount Everest was first reached in 1953 by Sir Edmund Hillary, a New Zealander, and Tenzing Norgay, a Sherpa. Sherpas are the native people of the mountainous region where Mount Everest lies. Since 1953, hundreds of people have climbed the peak and reached the summit. But more than one hundred forty have died before they reached the top. Yet over the years Mount Everest, and the surrounding mountains, have drawn increasingly large numbers of tourists.

Tourists who journey to see and climb Everest buy food and fuel, and hire guides, giving local people much-needed income. But so many visitors are coming that, high on Mount Everest, the ground is littered with hundreds of metal oxygen bottles, climbing and camping gear, and other garbage. At these high altitudes, few people have the energy to carry anything but themselves down the mountain. Many abandon gear that is not essential for their descent. In addition, in the dry, cold air, natural decay is slow so even the garbage really piles up.

Surrounding Everest, deforestation—the cutting and removal of trees—is a major problem. Over the years, many Nepalese have stripped the mountainside of trees, using the wood for heating homes and cooking food. Once the trees are gone, rain turns the mountainsides to mud, causing dangerous mudslides. Tourist lodges and expeditions are adding to the deforestation problem by using a lot of wood. So today visitors to Sagarmatha National Park, which encompasses Mount Everest, are required to bring their own fuel, such as kerosene, for expeditions. This eliminates some of the need for wood.

MEET ASIA'S OTHER MOUNTAINS

The continent of Asia has plenty of high points other than the Himalayas. Its tall mountain ranges include the Altai, Elburz, Hindu Kush, Karakoram, Kunlun Shan, the Pamirs, Qilian Shan, Qin Ling, Stanovoy, Tien Shan, Yablonovy, and Zagros. Because of their height, and snowcapped grandeur, the Pamirs and nearby plateaus—raised, table-like lands—are often called the "roof of the world." The Pamirs, located mostly in Tajikistan, form a hub where many of Asia's mountains converge. From the Pamirs, Asia's mountains extend in three directions. A broad belt curves northeast all the way to the cold eastern tip of Russia—the Chukchi Peninsula in the Arctic Ocean. Another belt curves south then west, through Iran toward Turkey. Still another belt of mountains curves from the Pamirs through the Himalayas and into southeast Asia.

In Tajikistan, vibrant flowers brighten the landscape of an alpine grassland high in the Pamir mountain range.

MOUNTAIN ANIMALS AWAKE: SPRING AND SUMMER

Mountain animals and plants follow a seasonal rhythm. In the Tien Shan mountains of Central Asia, most animals lay low during winter, when temperatures are cold and food is scarce. But in spring the snow melts at lower altitudes. Trickling meltwater fills streams and waters mountain meadows. Grass grows. Wild tulips bloom. Chicken-size birds called Himalayan snowcocks make eerie whistles that pierce the mountain air. White-clawed bears, which are a blonder race of the brown bears we know as grizzlies, wake up from their winter sleep. While bears are out searching for their spring meals, Apollo butterflies flit through the air.

In spring, red marmots—furry, woodchuck-size squirrels—emerge from their burrows. Marmots spend eight months underground in hibernation, a state in which their breathing and heart rates slow, reducing their bodies' need for food. In spring and summer marmots eat, fatten up, and raise their young, before returning to their dens deep underground. Summer is a time of plenty. Flowers bloom. Foxes, which eat young marmots, also roam the high mountains, and golden eagles soar in the blue skies.

MOUNTAINS: FOOT TO PEAK

If you hike up a tall mountain, you'll notice the scenery changes as you climb. In the northern Tien Shan, you can begin your hike in a desert. Yet farther up a mountain, you could stroll among maple trees, wild apple trees, and rosebushes. Still higher on the mountainside, aspen and birch trees grow. Above, the trees are mostly spruces and dwarf junipers. Finally, you reach the tree line, the zone above which trees do not grow.

Above the tree line, grasses, poppies, globeflowers, and other plants bloom in alpine meadows. On the highest parts of the mountain, the rocky slopes are bare of plants. Permanent snow covers many of these peaks, which cradle glaciers made of snow that has built up over thousands of years. This icy scene is much like those much farther north, in the Arctic. By climbing a mountain, you have reached conditions very similar to ones thousands of miles to the north.

GOING UP!

In spring, mountain animals, which spend the winter at lower elevations, move higher up mountain slopes. This migration allows the animals to take advantage of the flush of new plant growth, revealed by melting snows. Ibex, a species of wild goat, climb up the mountains in summer. Predators, such as snow leopards, climb higher, too, to pursue mountain goats and wild sheep. Ibisbills, rare birds that are gray and white and black with curved red bills, spend the winter in the lowlands. But in spring they fly up into the Tien Shan to nest on pebbled ground near mountain streams. They wade in these cold streams, feeding on insects, crustaceans, and small fish.

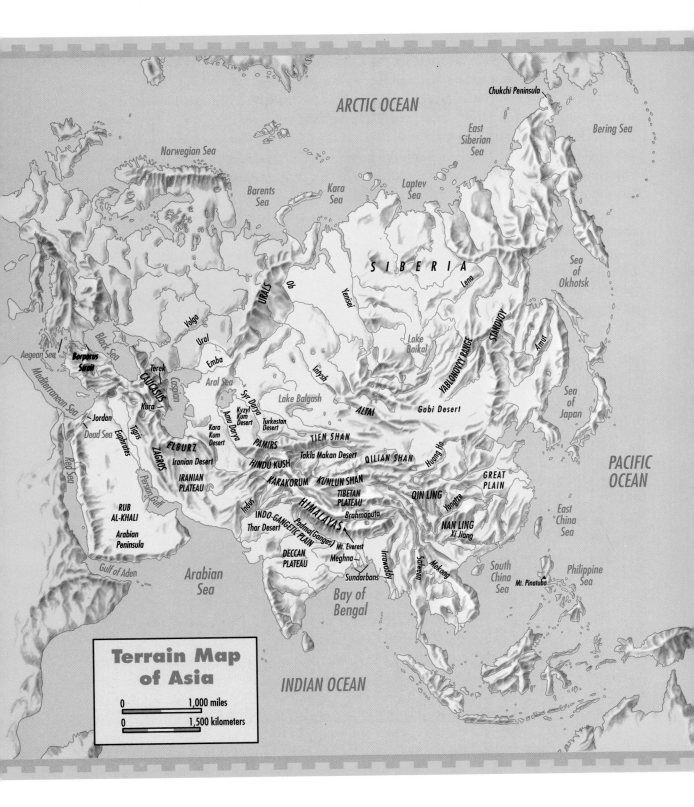

ARCTIC OCEAN

Chukchi Peninsula

East
Siberian
Sea

Bering Sea

Norwegian Sea

Barents
Sea

Kara
Sea

Laptev
Sea

Sea
of
Okhotsk

S I B E R I A

Lena

URALS

Ob

Yenisei

Amur

Volga

Ural

Lake
Baikal

YABLONOVYY RANGE

STANOVOY

Emba

Black Sea

Aegean Sea

Borporus
Strait

Terek

CAUCASUS

Caspian

Aral Sea

Lake Balgash

ALTAI

Gobi Desert

Sea
of
Japan

Mediterranean Sea

Kura

Syr Darya

Kyzyl
Kum
Desert

Turkestan
Desert

Jordan

Dead Sea

Tigris

Euphrates

ELBURZ

ZAGROS

Amu Darya

Kara
Kum
Desert

PAMIRS

TIEN SHAN

Irtysh

Huang Ho

PACIFIC
OCEAN

Red Sea

Iranian Desert

HINDU KUSH

Takla Makan Desert

QILIAN SHAN

GREAT
PLAIN

IRANIAN
PLATEAU

KARAKORUM

KUNLUN SHAN

QIN LING

East
China
Sea

RUB
AL-KHALI

Persian Gulf

Indus

INDO-GANGETIC PLAIN

Thar Desert

HIMALAYAS

Padma (Ganges)

TIBETAN
PLATEAU

Brahmaputra

Mt. Everest

Yangtze

NAN LING

Xi Jiang

Arabian
Peninsula

Gulf of Aden

DECCAN
PLATEAU

Meghna

Sundarbans

Irrawaddy

Salween

Mekong

South
China
Sea

Mt. Pinatubo

Philippine
Sea

Arabian
Sea

Bay of
Bengal

INDIAN OCEAN

Terrain Map of Asia

0   1,000 miles

0   1,500 kilometers

Care for some yak butter? You haven't truly experienced the mountains of Central Asia unless you've seen the yaks. Yaks are shaggy, horned cattle that once lived wild in the Himalayas. Now yaks are herded throughout the mountains of Central Asia by nomads—people who move from place to place.

The local people use yaks for meat and milk, some of which is made into butter. Yaks also carry loads. The yaks' long fur is terrific insulation against the winter cold—and not only for the yaks. Their fur is made into clothing. Even the yaks' droppings, called dung, can be burned for fuel when dry.

In addition to yaks, Central Asia's mountains are home to wild goats and wild sheep. Wild goats such as markhors have twisted horns; Siberian ibex have horns that are gently curved. The world's largest sheep, the argali, stands 4 feet (1.2 meters) high at the shoulder and has long, spiraled horns. Marco Polo sheep and blue sheep inhabit the mountains, too. Another famous mountain dweller is the giant panda, which lives in the bamboo forests of the Qin Ling mountains in China.

Yaks provide milk ten months of the year, and are the primary source of milk and dairy products for central Asia's nomadic people.

Steep, jagged mountains are not the only high places in Asia. Much of Asia consists of uplands—hills and small mountains. Uplands, much lower in height than the Himalayas, cover eastern Kazakhstan, eastern China, parts of Siberia, and islands such as Taiwan and Ceylon. Plateaus are another high elevation landform. The Deccan Plateau, a triangular plateau, makes up most of southern India. The Iranian Plateau sets the scene for the Iranian deserts. The most famous Asian plateau, the Tibetan Plateau, is a high, dry, relatively flat area surrounded by some of Asia's tallest mountains. Five times the area of California, the Tibetan Plateau has an average elevation of 15,000 feet (4,572 meters).

Life on the Tibetan Plateau

The Tibetan Plateau is dry because the Himalayas block the rains from the south. Yet despite this dryness, grass grows and people graze goats, sheep, yaks, and horses on the plateau. They ride horses or Bactrian camels, and spend nights in gers, small round tents.

The northern part of the plateau is a cold, windy, grassland wilderness, called the Chang Tang. There, wild yaks graze, lynx hunt, and Tibetan woolly hares munch on low-growing flowers. Vast herds of chirus, a kind of antelope with long, slender, ribbed horns, migrate across the plateau. Wolves hunt not only the chirus but also yaks, blue sheep, and pikas—mouselike relatives of rabbits.

In 1993, China declared the vast grassland a wilderness preserve, making it one of the earth's largest protected areas. Setting aside this region is one sign that people are beginning to recognize the value of wild, windy, cold places such as those found in Asia.

THREE

DESERT LANDS, DESERT LAKES, DESERT ISSUES

Asia contains a great variety of deserts—dry, mostly barren lands. Tremendous sand dunes, rose-colored mountains, and pebbled ground stretch mile after mile. Dry air, strong winds, sizzling hot summer temperatures, and swirling dust storms make these places difficult for plants and animals to live in. Yet desert dwellers such as mice, lizards, gazelles, wild cats, and camels somehow manage to survive.

WHY SO DRY?

Deserts receive less than 10 inches (25 centimeters) of rain per year. But most of Asia's deserts receive much less. Their extreme dryness is caused by several different factors. The Thar Desert of India and the Arabian Peninsula deserts are located in the subtropics, the latitudes near the tropics. These deserts are kept dry by large masses of air that descend at these latitudes and warm up, drying out the land. Other Asian deserts—the Iranian, Turkestan, Takla Makan, and Gobi—are dry because they are far from the ocean's moisture. In some cases, tall mountains also prevent moisture from reaching deserts.

DESERTS HOT AND COLD

Asia has two kinds of deserts: hot and cold. Hot deserts, such as the Thar and Arabian Peninsula deserts, are very hot in summer, with temperatures up to 129°F (54°C). Yet they are cold in winter, with temperatures reaching as low as freezing, 32°F (0°C). Cold deserts are still hot in summer but can get much, much colder in winter. The Gobi, in China, sizzles with summer temperatures of 113°F (45°C) but has winter temperatures as low as –40°F (–40°C)! Other cold Asian deserts include the Turkestan, Iranian, and Takla Makan. Cold deserts have what's called a continental climate, because this kind of climate is always found in the interior of a continent, far from an ocean. Places with a continental climate have a big difference between their cold winter temperatures and their hot summer temperatures. Deserts also heat up quickly during the day and cool off quickly at night.

In contrast, coastal regions experience less of a difference in temperature, from day to night, and season to season. Water is the key ingredient. It takes a lot of added heat, or heat loss, to change the temperature of water. So ocean water and moist ocean air tend to warm up and cool off slowly. This, in turn, slows down or even prevents radical changes in temperature for miles around.

THE AWESOME ARABIAN PENINSULA

The Rub'al-Khali, a section of the Arabian Peninsula's desert, is known for its tremendous sand dunes, some reaching 800 feet (240 meters) high. Other parts of the peninsula have flat, gravel-covered ground. There are no major rivers. But the peninsula does have aquifers—layers of porous, water-holding rock deep under ground. These aquifers naturally store rain that has fallen over thousands of years, or rain that has fallen in wetter regions, and flowed through the rock to drier regions. Where these aquifers are close to the surface, oases form, and date palm trees, the source of the date fruit, thrive. When rain arrives, it fills wadis—streambeds that are usually dry. Wildflowers and grasses sprout and quickly grow. Along the wadis, deep-rooted trees such as tamarinds can survive. But otherwise, plants are scarce. Scorpions, lizards, beetles, foxes, jackals, bearded vultures, and antelope called oryx live in the Arabian deserts, which are located in Saudi Arabia, Kuwait, Qatar, United Arab Emirates, Oman, and Yemen. Asir, a park in Saudi Arabia, preserves 1 million acres (400,000 hectares) of this spectacular desert.

CAMELS: SHIPS OF THE DESERT

Native to the deserts of Asia, camels are the ultimate desert beasts. Long legs keep a camel's body above the hot desert sand and its head above much of the blowing dust. When sand and dust storms do kick up, a camel can close its nostrils to keep dust out of its lungs. Thick fur insulates the camel's body, helping keep it warm on cold nights, and cool on hot days. And then, of course, there are the camel's famous humps, which help it survive as much as ten days without water.

Camel humps aren't full of water. They are full of fat. This fat, when used by the camel's body, produces not only energy, but water, as well. When a camel has gone without water for a while, its hump or humps actually become soft and sag! The one-

A domestic Bactrian camel is set out to graze in the Altai Mountains of Mongolia. Wild Bactrian camels live in the nearby Gobi Desert.

humped camel, called the dromedary, is found on the Arabian Peninsula. The two-humped, Bactrian camel is common in the rest of Asia. Almost all camels are domesticated today; only a thousand or so wild ones roam the Gobi Desert.

DIVE INTO A DESERT SEA

In Egypt, you can walk off sandy beaches backed by dry, brown desert, dive down into the Red Sea, and find a colorful surprise. Under the waters of the Red Sea, just offshore from the Arabian Peninsula's dry deserts, are coral reefs, brimming with fish, corals, anemones, and eels.

Twenty-five million years ago, the Red Sea did not exist. But then a crack formed in the tectonic plates that carried Africa. New sea floor began oozing out. The Arabian Peninsula, once part of Africa, split away, moving along with Asia. Today the Red Sea is getting wider and wider, by about 1 inch (2.5 centimeters) a year. Some day the Red Sea may be as large as the Atlantic Ocean! Currently, the Red Sea is fairly isolated from the rest of the ocean. Its only natural connection to the ocean is a narrow strait, leading to the Gulf of Aden and the Indian Ocean. Because of this, many Red Sea creatures have evolved separately, and differently, from animals in the rest of the world's oceans. Twenty percent of the Red Sea's animals are endemic, meaning they are found nowhere else on earth!

THE THAR DESERT: A HOPPING PLACE

Hopping through the sands of the Thar Desert is an animal you might recognize. Gerbils—similar to the ones you see in pet stores—live wild in this region and many other Asian deserts. Gerbils stay in underground burrows during the heat of the day. In the cool of the evening they emerge to eat the sparse grass. Like the Arabian Peninsula deserts, the Thar Desert of India and Pakistan is a hot desert. It is also one of Asia's wettest. In some years, the Thar receives 8 inches (21 centimeters) of rain. Using this water, acacia, salt cedar, and caper bushes can grow. The grazing of goats, sheep, and camels in this desert strongly affects what plants thrive. The animals eat plant leaves and churn up the soil with their hooves, crushing small plants. Only plants that can endure these conditions survive. Thar wildlife includes wild asses, a kind of antelope called blackbuck, and blue bulls, a bluish-gray grazing animal.

TAKLA MAKAN: DUNES AND MORE DUNES

The Takla Makan Desert, in northwestern China, is a great place to see sand dunes shift and change. A layer of sand 1,000 feet (300 meters) thick forms dunes shaped like crescents, crosses, and stars. The Takla Makan gets so little rain that bushes, reeds, and trees only grow along its rivers. Not surprisingly, animals are more plentiful near water, too. If you're lucky you might see a wolf, a sand fox, a wild boar, a deer, or perhaps even a Bactrian camel. Other desert dwellers include scorpions, sand eels, larks, hedgehogs, hares, and jerboas—small rodents that hop like kangaroos.

TURKESTAN: HOME TO WILD CATS

Roaming the Turkestan Desert are some really wild cats: spotted wild cats, dune cats, and desert lynx. Cats, in fact, are a major predator in many of Asia's deserts. They eat ground squirrels, desert hares, and other small mammals. Animals, however, are few and far between in the desert. You are more likely to see plants, such as wormwood, saltbush, or saxaul. After rains, the desert blooms with colorful tulips; but usually it is just bare sand.

The Turkestan Desert, which is located in Kazakhstan, Uzbekistan, and Turkmenistan, is made up of two poetic-sounding sections: the Kara Kum, and the Kyzyl Kum. The Kara Kum, meaning black sand, has gray sand dunes and lies south of the Kyzyl Kum, which means red sand. Less sandy, the Kyzyl Kum contains features such as

Workers use heavy equipment on an irrigation project in the Kyzyl Kum.
Irrigation is necessary in order to grow crops in the region.

takyrs, which are bare clay spots, and inselbergs, strangely shaped landforms that jut up as much as 3,000 feet (900 meters) above the surrounding desert. Both the Kara Kum and the Kyzyl Kum experience weather extremes, with temperatures as cold as −44°F (−42°C) in winter and as warm as 120°F (49°C) in summer.

THE SHRINKING ARAL SEA

Despite its name, the Aral Sea is really a salty lake. Located just east of the Kyzyl Kum, the Aral Sea was once one of the world's largest lakes, supporting a fishing industry and busy ports. But now the Aral Sea is dying, drying up in the desert sun.

Each year more and more of the Aral's shore is exposed. The remaining water is getting saltier as water evaporates, leaving salt behind. Almost all the Aral Sea's twenty-four species of fish have died. Ships have been left stranded in the sand. The port city of Aral'sk, once on the shore, is now located more than 30 miles (48 kilometers) from the water!

The shrinking of the Aral Sea began in 1960, when the Soviet Union began taking water out of the Syr Darya and Amu Darya rivers, to irrigate rice and cotton crops.

Ships stranded by the Aral Sea's receding waters litter the sand.

These two rivers feed the Aral Sea. Without their constant inflow, the Aral's water evaporates and is not replenished. The lake surface has shrunk by almost a third since the irrigation projects began. Strong winds are blowing dust and salt from the exposed lake bottom onto nearby land, ruining crops.

Restoring the Aral Sea to its former size is probably impractical. But in 1993 concerned citizens of the region set up the International Fund to Save the Aral Sea. They are working with the United Nations Environment Program and local governments to stop further shrinking of the Aral Sea and restore the regional environment.

TREASURE UNDER A DESERT LAKE

Located next to the Aral Sea, the Caspian Sea—another lake—has always been a source of wealth. Living in the sea are sturgeon, huge fish whose eggs, called Russian caviar, are eaten as a gourmet delicacy. A full-grown sturgeon can weigh 2,000 pounds (907 kilograms). Its eggs can be worth hundreds of thousands of dollars! Today, however, the rush is on for other wealth—oil—that lies under the Caspian Sea. Underneath its waters lie an estimated 10 to 16 percent of the world's oil reserves, up to 200 billion barrels of

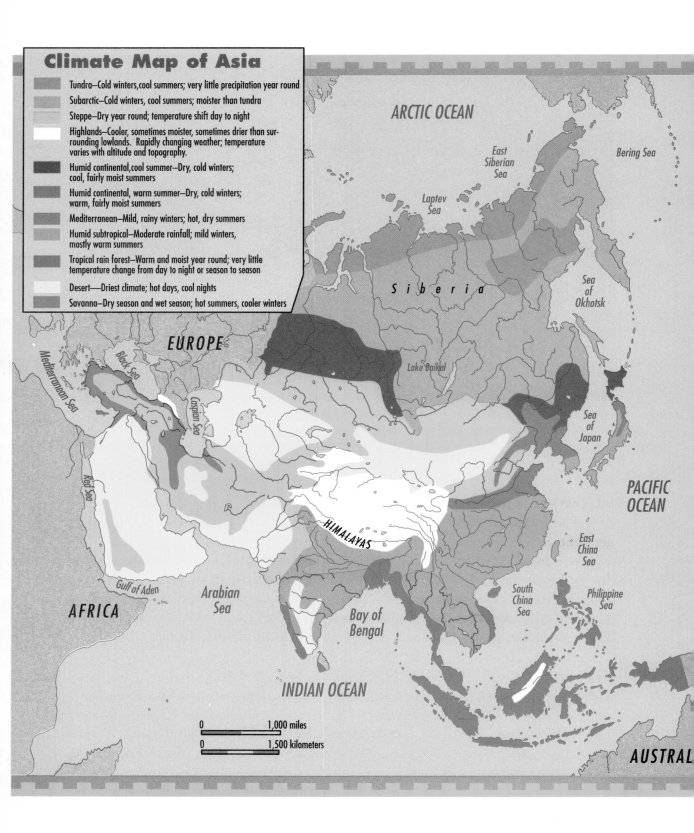

Climate Map of Asia

Tundra—Cold winters, cool summers; very little precipitation year round

Subarctic—Cold winters, cool summers; moister than tundra

Steppe—Dry year round; temperature shift day to night

Highlands—Cooler, sometimes moister, sometimes drier than sur-rounding lowlands. Rapidly changing weather; temperature varies with altitude and topography.

Humid continental, cool summer—Dry, cold winters; cool, fairly moist summers

Humid continental, warm summer—Dry, cold winters; warm, fairly moist summers

Mediterranean—Mild, rainy winters; hot, dry summers

Humid subtropical—Moderate rainfall; mild winters, mostly warm summers

Tropical rain forest—Warm and moist year round; very little temperature change from day to night or season to season

Desert—Driest climate; hot days, cool nights

Savanna—Dry season and wet season; hot summers, cooler winters

ARCTIC OCEAN

Bering Sea

East Siberian Sea

Laptev Sea

Sea of Okhotsk

Siberia

Lake Baikal

Sea of Japan

EUROPE

Black Sea

Caspian Sea

Mediterranean Sea

Red Sea

HIMALAYAS

PACIFIC OCEAN

East China Sea

Gulf of Aden

Arabian Sea

Bay of Bengal

South China Sea

Philippine Sea

AFRICA

INDIAN OCEAN

0   1,000 miles

0   1,500 kilometers

AUSTRAL

*People enjoying the Caspian seashore are dwarfed by
the oil rigs that fill the horizon.*

oil. That's three trillion dollars worth of oil, at least, so it's no wonder the border countries of Russia, Iran, Kazakhstan, Turkmenistan, and Azerbaijan are negotiating hard to get rights to large portions of the oil.

The Caspian Sea is the largest inland body of water in the world. It covers an area of 143,205 square miles (371,000 square kilometers), making it about the size of Montana and more than four times the size of Lake Superior. Fed by the Volga, Ural, Emba, Terek, and Kura rivers, the Caspian Sea has no outlet to the ocean.

As oil-hungry nations compete to carve up oil rights in the Caspian Sea, environmentalists are voicing their concerns. The water level of the Caspian has already fallen, as water has been diverted for crops. With pollution from oil drilling a potential problem as well, can the sturgeon and other creatures of the Caspian Sea survive? No one knows.

IRANIAN DESERT

If you are walking in the Iranian desert, watch where you step. Not just because of the snakes and scorpions, but mostly because of the slime. Thick salt, the remnant of dried-up lakes, covers much of the ground. But soft mud lies below the salt crust. People, camels, and jeeps sometimes get stuck in this slime. Even with the slime, the Iranian desert is a beautiful place, with rose-colored mountains, huge salt flats, and salt-covered ground, sparkling in the sun. Thorny shrubs, acacia trees, and tamarisk trees grow near oases and along irrigation tunnels dug by the Iranians. When it does rain in this desert, wildflowers sprout, grasses grow, and rabbits, gazelles, gerbils, jerboas, and other plant eaters fill the landscape. When food is scarce, the squirrels, gerbils, and other rodents hibernate in underground burrows.

BIG AND COLD: THE GOBI DESERT

Asia's largest desert, the Gobi, is more than three times the size of the state of California. Located in China and Mongolia, the desert is surrounded on three sides by mountains. Unlike the Arabian Peninsula deserts, the Gobi has very few sand dunes. Most of it is stony desert, a surface made of small pebbles with even tinier bits of sand in between. Over time, dust and moisture give the stones a dark sheen, called desert varnish.

Plants are generally small, few, and far between, except along rivers. Gobi wildlife includes grasshoppers, lizards, beetles, eagles, sand grouse, jerboas, gerbils, saiga antelope, Chinese desert cats, Pallas's cats, and three kinds of gazelles. But the Gobi is perhaps best known as the last home of the Przewalski's horse. The horse is named for

Once found running wild in the Gobi Desert, Przewalski's horses are now found only in captivity. This photograph was taken at the Central Park Zoo in New York City.

Nikolai Przhevalski, a Russian explorer who traveled widely, collecting plants and animals throughout Russia. He discovered the yellow-bodied, black-maned, pony-size horses, which were the last truly wild horses. Most other wild horses are descendants of domestic horses that have escaped. Wild Przewalski's horses have not been seen in a long time. They are suspected to have died out in the wild. But some survive in zoos.

DESERT LAND, DESERT ISSUES

In Asia, particularly in the Middle East, many people live in deserts, semideserts, and dry grasslands. They depend on water from rivers such as the Jordan, Tigris, and Euphrates for drinking and bathing, watering cattle and crops, and for running industry. These days, however, the number of people in the Middle East is rising, water use is increasing, and the amount of water available to each person is decreasing, rapidly.

Jordan, Israel, Syria, Saudi Arabia, and other Middle Eastern countries share the same rivers and aquifers. Governments and people want this water not only for daily needs, but also to produce electricity. For example, the Atatürk Dam in Turkey holds back part of the Euphrates River, and the water's energy is harnessed to produce electricity.

The Ataturk Dam, found on the Euphrates River, is a source of hydroelectric power for the people of Turkey.

THE GREAT GREEN WALL

In inner Mongolia, the northern part of China near the country of Mongolia, wind pushes sand dunes over croplands, smothering them. So, since 1978, China has been planting a huge band of trees that stretches over eleven provinces. People have nicknamed the project the "Great Green Wall." This name is derived from China's famous Great Wall, an ancient, 25-foot (7.6-meter) high wall, 1,500 miles (2,400 kilometers) long, that was built to keep invaders out of the country. The purpose of the Great Green Wall is for the trees to keep the sand in place and help prevent the sand dunes from blowing over farmers' fields. So far, the technique is working. Keeping deserts in their place is a priority because the growing population of Asia desperately needs agricultural land.

WHEN WATER IS SCARCE

Water shortages make life difficult for many people in the Middle East. People carry buckets of water long distances to their houses or to their crops. Or they must spend their hard-earned money to buy water from passing water trucks. Without water for washing, disease is more easily spread, and serious epidemics can occur.

Middle Easterners are taking many different approaches to solving their water problems. Some farmers conserve water by covering crops with plastic. Many use drip irrigation, laying pipes with holes in them along the ground, in order to drip water directly onto the soil instead of spraying it. This technique reduces the amount of water that is lost to evaporation. Countries such as Kuwait and Saudi Arabia obtain water by removing the salt from seawater. This process, called desalinization, is effective, but can be expensive.

No matter what their religion, or nationality, the people of the Middle East are linked by their need for water. Sharing it can be a challenge. When one person digs a well, and uses underground water, the level of water goes down. Another person's well may go dry. When a farmer diverts a stream to water his or her crops, the people downstream may have little water to drink. In the Middle East, which has been torn by wars over politics, religion, history, and ownership of land, water scarcity could be another source of future conflict—or an opportunity to work together, diplomatically.

FOUR

RIVERS—THE LIFE OF ASIA

In Asia, where much of the climate is dry, rivers are the life of the land. Rivers form lush green ribbons in dry brown landscapes and provide water for irrigating crops. Flooding rivers spread out over the land, in both dry and wet climates, depositing nutrient-rich mud that helps farmers grow food. Flooding also creates wetlands that are important animal habitats.

The primary rivers of Asia are the Amu Darya, Amur, Brahmaputra, Euphrates, Ganges, Huang Ho, Indus, Irrawaddy, Irtysh, Lena, Mekong, Ob', Salween, Tigris, Xi Jiang, Yangtze, and Yenisei rivers. These rivers vary from cold, fast-flowing rivers churning through narrow canyons to warm, slow-moving rivers that spread out over the land. Wherever they flow, rivers change the surrounding landscape, and form watery highways for people and wildlife.

WHERE RIVERS START

You probably know that most rivers eventually flow to the sea, pouring their water into the ocean. But have you ever thought about where rivers begin? The region where a river begins is called its headwaters. In Asia most rivers' headwaters are in the mountains. The Mekong, Indus, Brahmaputra, Salween, and Ganges rivers all start high in the mountains of Tibet, India, and China, mostly in the Himalayan range. These mountain rivers begin as melting snow and ice, primarily from glaciers. The Yangtze River and the Yellow River begin in the Kunlun Mountains of China. To the north another Asian river, the Yenisei-Angara, begins in a lake, instead: Lake Baikal.

All these rivers start small. But then melting snow and falling rain add to their volume. Tributaries—streams and rivers that pour into the main river—increase the rivers' volume, as well. By the time these rivers join other rivers, or pour into the Indian, Arctic, or Pacific oceans, they are powerful, and wide.

LIVING ALONG THE MEKONG

Imagine living in a house that stands on stilts or paddling a boat to the market, where you buy your vegetables from other people's canoes. You might do these things and more if you lived in southeast Asia, along the Mekong River, a 2,600-mile (4,194-kilometer) river that flows from China into Vietnam. On the Mekong, some families live in floating houses. They raise catfish in cages suspended under their houses, feeding the fish by dropping food through a trapdoor in the living room floor! When the fish are big enough, the family can eat them or sell them to support themselves.

The Mekong begins in China, on the high, cold Tibetan Plateau. From there, it flows past parts of Myanmar (Burma), Laos, Thailand, Cambodia, and Vietnam. Along the way, it runs by fields of peanuts and cabbages, and fields of rice called paddies. It also flows through the jungle of Laos. Giant fruit bats, ducks, frogs, fish-hunting birds called

Traffic is heavy at this on-the-water market on Vietnam's Mekong River. Fresh produce and other goods are available at river markets throughout Southeast Asia.

kingfishers, and other creatures live in and along the Mekong. One native fish, the giant catfish, can weigh 650 pounds (295 kilograms)!

Compared to other major Asian rivers, the Mekong is relatively natural and free flowing. It winds past only one big city, and has very few dams or bridges. But despite its isolation, the Mekong is not a wilderness river, untouched by human activities. The Mekong and forests along its shores are still recovering from damage that occurred during World War II, the Vietnam War, and other warfare in the region. In the 1960s, during the Vietnam War, the United States military sprayed the surrounding forests with Agent Orange, a herbicide, which kills plants, including trees, causing their leaves to drop. The purpose of doing this was to find Communist soldiers who were hiding in the forest. Agent Orange contains dioxin, a long-lasting, cancer-causing chemical that is still present in the river, in the soil, and in many people who live near the river. Dioxin in the plants was passed to aquatic insects that ate the dying plants, to fish that ate the insects, and to people who ate the fish. Dioxin contamination is a long-term problem for parts of the Mekong. But despite the presence of dioxin, some forests have regrown along the river's banks and people are working to reforest the land.

MUDDIEST RIVER IN THE WORLD: CHINA'S HUANG HO

Flowing through northern China and Mongolia is a strange river. Its water level is higher than the surrounding land. Dikes—barriers made of stone, rope, steel cable, and plants—line the river, keeping the water from spilling out onto surrounding farm fields. This river, called the Yellow River, or Huang Ho, is the muddiest on earth. More than half of the river's weight is mud, making the Huang Ho look more like soup than river water. The yellow silt—tiny rock particles—it carries gives the river both its color and its name.

The Huang Ho flows through China's Great Plain, which is covered by loess—loose dirt particles deposited there by wind. The loess, which can be 3,000 feet (1,000 meters) thick, comes primarily from the Gobi Desert. Loess is fertile and good for farming, when irrigated. So the Great Plain is densely populated with farmers. But living near the river is dangerous, because it floods and changes course easily and often. At times, disastrous floods have killed hundreds of thousands of people on China's Great Plain.

HOLDING BACK THE FLOODS

For 4,000 years, the people of China have tried to control the Huang Ho. They have walled in the river channel with dikes so the water does not usually spill over into fields. Unfortunately, this solution has caused long-term problems. Trapped in the channel, the river cannot flood and deposit its silt. So the mud deposits on the riverbed. Year after year, silt builds the river higher and the river's water level rises. People, in turn, have to build the dikes higher to contain the water. The raised river and raised dikes create a dangerous situation. When rains are heavy, strong floods can occur, breaking the dikes and letting the water run free.

CHINA'S ENORMOUS NEW DAM

Flowing east to west across central China, the Yangtze River, the 4th longest river in the world, will soon enter the record books in another category. This river, also called the Chang Jiang, or long river, will soon be the site of a dam of mind-boggling size. The Three Gorges Dam, scheduled to be completed in 2009, will produce 18,200 megawatts of electricity—as much as eighteen nuclear power plants—and more than any other dam. The dam itself will be more than 1 mile (1.6 kilometers) wide. Behind it, water will collect in a reservoir covering a 253-square-mile (632-square-kilometer) area. There will be so much water in this reservoir that some scientists are concerned the weight of the water could cause the ground to shift, creating earthquakes.

Hydroelectric dams such as Three Gorges produce electricity by harnessing the force of flowing water. The river water flows through turbines, which are fanlike machines. These turn like waterwheels and convert the water's energy to electricity. The Chinese government, which is funding the project (at a price tag of $30 billion or more) says the dam and related construction will not only produce electricity, but also help control flooding in the region. Government sources also maintain that, in addition, the electricity the dam generates may help reduce the use of coal-burning power plants. These plants currently spew out air pollution, which blankets parts of China.

THE DEVASTATING COST OF THE DAM

Despite its potential advantages, the dam will have a terrible cost, to both people and the environment. When the dam is constructed, and the reservoir fills in, large valleys will be underwater. More than a million people will have to move to new areas, as the water engulfs 1,500 towns and villages. The people of the region are being paid a small sum for their land, and some are being resettled in new cities built for this purpose. But it is difficult for them to leave. Many of these people will leave behind the homes they and their ancestors have inhabited for six hundred years or more. The reservoir will drown a tremendous natural area, eliminating the length of river that was in that area. This, in turn, will reduce habitat for rare fish and the Chinese river dolphin. The reservoir will also cover valuable archaeological sites.

Critics of the dam include some Chinese citizens, international human rights activists, and international environmental groups. They dismiss government claims that the dam will reduce air pollution, because China's energy needs are growing so rapidly that all available energy, from the dam and coal-burning plants, is likely to be used in the future. Critics are also concerned about pollution of the river and reservoir. China has

A young girl watches the construction of the Three Gorges Dam. More than a million people will have to be relocated before the dam is completed in 2009.

very few sewage treatment plants, so a lot of sewage will run into the reservoir. And the water behind the dam will flow over old factories, full of toxic chemicals, that are being submerged.

THE FUTURE OF THE YANGTZE

To offset such criticism, the Chinese government has announced plans to build twenty waste water treatment plants to prevent sewage from running into the reservoir. They have also pledged to reduce the use of toxic chemicals along the river. The Chinese government is planning to spend millions of dollars to plant trees along the riverbanks, too. This will help reduce soil erosion caused by the construction, and prevent heavy rains from washing soil into the river and reservoir. But critics of the dam still feel the building of the Three Gorges Dam will be one of the worst environmental disasters ever. And so, like many other rivers in Asia, the future of the Yangtze is uncertain, as human demands for water and electricity rise.

FIVE

MAKE WAY FOR MONSOONS: THE INDIAN SUBCONTINENT

About 55 million years ago, the Indian Subcontinent—a region now known as India, Bangladesh, and Pakistan—slammed into the continent of Asia. The force of the impact pushed up the Himalayas. The Himalayas continue slowly rising, even to this day. Now a part of Asia, the Indian Subcontinent is protected from cool northern air by the tall Himalayas. But this warm region experiences powerful shifts in weather conditions and occasional, deadly storms from the south. Each year, the lives of plants, animals, and people in the Indian Subcontinent depend on when the rain comes, where the winds blow, and how much the rivers rise during the rains.

MONSOONS SHAPE THE LIFE OF INDIA

In India, in May, near the end of the hot season, it feels like every person and every animal is waiting for rain. The air is dry and extremely hot, as much as 120°F (49°C). Muddy ground dries and cracks. Dust settles on plates, on dishes, on clothes. Water can be scarce. Tempers can flare and people can feel crabby because it's hard to sleep in the heat.

Relief comes with the monsoon, a seasonal shift of winds that brings rain to the Indian Subcontinent. A monsoon begins forming when the land heats up during the hot season. The air over the land heats up, too, and rises. Cool, wet ocean air slowly moves in to replace the hot rising air. When this happens, the monsoon rains begin.

The rain marks the beginning of India's wet season, one of three distinct seasons: the hot, the wet, and the cool. The hot, the period before the monsoons, lasts from February through May. The wet, the time of the monsoon, usually begins in June, although sometimes the rains come late or not at all. During the wet, from June to September, it rains almost every day. At first temperatures remain high, but eventually fall. From October to late January is the cool season, when the land is green and lush and the air has lost its heat.

WELCOMING THE RAIN

Peacocks, which are native to India, begin to court and call just before the monsoon rains. The male spreads his tail feathers, shakes them, and struts around. The female, duller in color, chooses the male with the showiest feather display. When people see peacocks doing their mating display, they know the monsoon should begin soon.

The arrival of the monsoon is a time of joyous celebration. People stand in flooded streets, soaked by the rains, smiling and shouting prayers of thanks for the monsoon's return. The monsoon rains begin on the southern tip of India, working their way northwest. But once the monsoon clouds are inland, they can shift, watering one farmer's field and not an adjacent one. Without the rain, farmers' crops fail.

After the heat, the rain is a relief, and the air temperature gradually drops. Moisture brings life to the land. Crops and gardens grow lush. Rice farmers plant and tend their crops. But living with the drenching rain is not always easy. People have difficulty driving and bicycling through the flooded areas. Fishing boats cannot go out onto the stormy seas. Rain pours into places where snakes usually hide, so the snakes emerge, posing a danger to humans.

Almost all the rain the region gets for the year will fall in the four months of the monsoon season. The town of Mawsynram, in northeast India, is the rainiest place on earth. It gets 467.44 inches (1,187 centimeters) of rain per year. Even so, the townspeople cope with the weather. The monsoon rains are part of a seasonal cycle of life. As such, they are something to welcome, to celebrate, and sometimes complain about, just like the spring, summer, fall, and winter seasons experienced by people who live elsewhere.

TRANSFORMING THE LAND

From the forested mountains of western India to the low-lying Ganges plains, animals breed and raise young during the monsoon season. Frogs that spend most of the year underground come out of their burrows to breed and lay eggs in the puddles created by the monsoons. The hot weather just before the monsoon rains also triggers the hatching of gharial crocodile eggs. Later, the young gharials spread out, swimming along flooded rivers, to colonize new places. Monsoon flooding creates large wetlands where storks, herons, egrets, cormorants, and other birds nest. Full of fish and frogs, the wetlands are an important source of food for birds feeding their chicks. Painted storks will not breed if the monsoon rains do not reach their nesting grounds. Instead, they will just wait for the next year!

EXPLORING THE INDO-GANGETIC PLAIN

Just south of the Himalayas is a vast apron of low-lying land called the Indo-Gangetic Plain. This region, which stretches from Pakistan to India to Bangladesh, is made of mud and sand carried by rivers down from the Himalayas over thousands of years. The thick mud and sand layer give the area some of the deepest and most fertile soils on earth. Three river systems, the Indus, Brahmaputra, and Ganges, also spread out over the land, creating soggy areas where wet grasslands and mangrove swamps thrive.

GRASS THAT COULD HIDE AN ELEPHANT

In India's Kaziranga National Park, some grasses grow to almost 20 feet (6 meters) tall. So it's difficult at first to see the wildlife. Tourists, however, can get a better view from the backs of domestic elephants, elephants raised in captivity and trained to carry people. While riding elephants, visitors may see leopards, swamp deer, hog deer, wild elephants, wild buffalo, or the rare one-horned rhinoceroses. It's best not to get too close to rhinos. Although they are plant eaters, rhinos are dangerous and may charge!

Tourists can see above the tall grass and snap photographs of wildlife while riding on elephants in Kaziranga National Park.

MAN-EATING TIGERS AND MARVELOUS MANGROVES

In the Sundarbans, the world's largest mangrove swamp, people are not the only large predators. The local Bengal tigers sometimes hunt humans. The huge cats swim up to small boats and carry away full-grown men, then kill them and eat them. Such behavior is extremely rare for tigers that live elsewhere. (Tigers usually feed on boars, monkeys called macaques, monitor lizards, and birds.) But in the Sundarbans, which stretches from India into Bangladesh, 30 to 150 people are killed by tigers each year on the Indian side of the border. Tigers in the Sundarbans are good swimmers. They have to be, because mangrove swamps are flooded most of the time. Mangrove swamps are wetlands: part forest, part river, part ocean. They occur where rivers meet the sea.

A Bengal tiger carries off a fawn it has killed in India's Ranthambhore National Park.

Twenty different species of mangrove trees grow in the Sundarbans. Mangroves are adapted to live half in, half out of the water. Wet, tide-washed soil is not very stable, so mangroves send out prop roots. These curved side roots prop them up, so the trees don't fall over. As mangroves send out roots and spread, they help create new land. Their roots hold the soil in place, and mud and sand fills in behind them. Young mangrove trees form on the parent plant, then drop into the water. The young plants can float to new areas, take root, and grow.

MUDSKIPPERS AND MORE

Mangroves are home to lots of different animals. When the tide is low, fiddler crabs crawl along the mud. Mudskippers—a type of fish—hop around, using their fins like feet. When the tide is higher and the forest is flooded, the area under the mangrove roots becomes a shallow nursery for young fish and shrimp. Up in the trees, storks, herons, egrets, and other waterbirds build nests. Crocodiles and monitor lizards hunt in the mangrove swamp. In addition to being an important wildlife habitat, and a nursery for fish, the mangroves help protect the mainland from big waves during storms. The roots and trees slow the water down and help hold the soil in place.

For decades, the people and government of India have recognized the value of wildlife and wild spaces. They have created more than 450 national parks. Special breeding programs help rare species such as gharial crocodiles and Asian lions survive.

Today, however, breeding programs and parks face financial cutbacks. And poachers—people who illegally hunt wildlife—are killing rhinos, tigers, crocodiles, and other animals for body parts. Tiger whiskers, tiger bones, rhino horns, crocodile skins, and other products are sold for use in Chinese medicine. Because of poaching and habitat loss, the tiger population has decreased drastically throughout Asia. Many tiger experts believe that there will be few, if any, wild tigers left in Asia in ten years.

Economic problems and poachers are not the only threats to India's wildlife. In India, like many other parts of the world, wood for fuel is scarce. People cut trees from parks to make charcoal for cooking food. People also illegally graze their goats, sheep, and cattle on parklands. India has the second largest human population of any country in the world. (China has the largest.) As this population increases, humans move closer and closer to parks and conflicts arise between people and wildlife. The threat to wildlife in India and other countries with rapidly growing populations is very grave indeed.

Near some parks, concerned citizens have formed groups to protect forests and wildlife. One, the Ranthambore Foundation, works on planting native trees around houses, creating oases where birds and other small animals can survive. Forest conservationists are working with herders to find new food sources, so that grazing animals do not need to come into the parks. These kinds of efforts will not solve the problems of preserving wildlife, but at least they are a start.

BANGLADESH: RIVER COUNTRY

Bangladesh is a country built by rivers. When river water meets the ocean, it slows down. Once it loses momentum, it cannot carry as much material. So it drops its load of sand and clay, forming a river delta, such as the one Bangladesh sits on. The Ganges, Padma, Meghna, and Jamuna (called Brahmaputra in India) rivers all flow through Bangladesh and help build its muddy coastline.

Bangladesh is one of the most crowded countries on earth. Many of its people make their homes on riverbanks and small islands in the paths of rivers. Some live in houseboats, or houses on stilts. Vast fields of rice make parts of the flooded land bright green.

Such a life, however, can be precarious. Each year, snow melting in the Himalayas, plus rain from the monsoons, make rivers rise. Swollen rivers jump their banks and carve out new channels. Rivers flood, covering as much as one fifth of Bangladesh with water. The low-lying river islands and riverbanks people live on often wash away.

The rivers of Bangladesh bring life to the country. The people need the river water. Rivers allow people to transport goods up and down its waterways. The soil deposited during floods fertilizes the land, making it good for growing crops such as rice, sugarcane, and jute, which is used for making burlap. But the river waters also bring disaster, at times, not only during devastating floods but also during tropical cyclones.

CYCLONES: A FACT OF LIFE

Tropical cyclones are large storms with strong winds that rotate around a central point. These storms are known as typhoons in the Pacific, hurricanes in the Atlantic, and simply as cyclones in the Indian Ocean. In 1991 an unusually strong tropical cyclone hit Bangladesh, killing 139,000 people and destroying 10 million homes. Hurricane-force winds flattened houses. Many of the dead were killed by storm surges, walls of ocean water and river water pushed inland by strong winds. Some people survived by climbing trees. But the best refuges were concrete buildings, which are structurally much stronger than the mud and grass homes inhabited by most Bangladeshis. Since 1991 the government of Bangladesh, with financial aid from other nations and private organizations, has built 1,275 concrete buildings, to serve as emergency shelters during cyclones, and as schools and community centers the rest of the year.

Scientists believe there may be a connection between the severity of cyclone damage and the loss of mangrove swamps over the years. Some mangroves have been cut down; others are dying because they are not receiving enough river water. The government of Bangladesh, with international assistance, is investing millions of dollars in changing water flow so that the mangroves receive the balance of freshwater and ocean water they need. Cyclones and monsoon rains are a fact of life in the Indian Subcontinent. They cannot be prevented. So people and animals must prepare and cope as best they can.

Concrete buildings offer the best protection from cyclones. But most people in Bangladesh live in flimsy structures that are easily crushed by these strong storms.

SIX

SOUTHEAST ASIA: FIERY BEGINNINGS, FABULOUS FORESTS

In August 1883 the volcanic island of Krakatoa erupted with the force of ten thousand atom bombs. The noise was so loud that people heard it hundreds of miles away. The explosion was so strong, it created tidal waves that hit nearby islands, killing tens of thousands of people. Two thirds of the island was destroyed. Dust from the explosion was carried 17 miles (27 kilometers) up into the air.

Krakatoa, one of Indonesia's islands, seemed entirely lifeless after the eruption. Nine months later, scientists looking for animals on the island found only one: a spider. Today, however, plants and animals that have floated, flown, and swum to Krakatoa from other islands are becoming established. Two hundred species of plants now grow on Krakatoa, including a developing tropical forest. More than seventy species of vertebrates—animals with backbones—live there, too.

The forests on Krakatoa are nowhere near as complex and colorful as tropical forests elsewhere in Southeast Asia. But scientists are watching the natural changes on the island with interest. Krakatoa is a living laboratory, teaching biologists how a forest begins, how island life develops, and how biodiversity evolves. It's one of many intriguing places in Southeast Asia that remind scientists they still have much to learn.

LIVING WITH VOLCANOES

Indonesia, which is made up of 17,000 islands, has more volcanoes than any other country in the world. Java, the largest and most populous island, is the size of New York State, yet it has seventeen active volcanoes! Earthquakes, too, are common in the region.

In July 1998 an earthquake measuring 7.1 on the Richter scale hit near New Guinea. The ocean floor moved, shifting down, then back up. This movement created a gigantic ocean wave, called a tsunami. The tsunami, more than 23 feet (7 meters) high, hit the coast of Papua New Guinea, destroying villages and killing several thousand people.

Indonesia's earthquakes and its volcanoes are caused by the motion of tectonic plates. Underneath Indonesia, one tectonic plate is sliding over another. As they jolt past each other, earthquakes occur. (The Java Trench, a tremendous 22,965-foot [7,000-meter] trench in the ocean floor, indicates the border where these two plates meet.) The friction of the plates rubbing against one another heats up the plates, partly melting them. This molten rock builds up under pressure and can erupt out of volcanoes as fiery hot lava. The lava, when cool, forms new land. Over time, underwater volcanoes can build up enough land to break the surface, creating new islands.

Other parts of southeastern and eastern Asia are prone to earthquakes and volcanic eruptions. In 1991 the Philippines' Mount Pinatubo erupted after six hundred years of inactivity. Fortunately, geologists were able to give people ample warning of the pending eruption, so most escaped the ash and mudslides. Hundreds of thousands of people were evacuated, 1.2 million homes were destroyed, and 800 people died. The Philippines, New Guinea, and to the north, Japan, are located within a network of volcanoes called the Pacific "ring of fire." These volcanoes border the Pacific tectonic plate.

Volcanic ash covers the Philippine countryside following the eruption of Mount Pinatubo in 1991.

When people mention Southeast Asia, they mean the mainland countries of Thailand, Malaysia, Laos, Cambodia, Vietnam, and Myanmar, plus the island countries of Indonesia, Singapore, and the Philippines. All these countries are located in the tropics, the area closest to the equator, so at sea level the air temperature is warm almost all the time. Indonesia, for instance, has an average temperature of 79°F (26°C) throughout the year. Rainfall in the tropics, however, varies. Some areas get 200 inches (500 centimeters) of rain each year, while others receive only a tenth as much. Near the equator, where tropical rain forest grows, rainfall arrives fairly evenly throughout the year. Farther from the equator, forests experience wet and dry seasons. They have a monsoon climate, much like the one in India. These areas cannot support tropical rain forests. Instead, they have monsoon forests, which have trees that drop their leaves during the dry season.

RAIN FOREST: LAYERS OF LIFE

Like tropical rain forests in South America, Asia's tropical rain forests have many layers of life. Exceptionally tall trees, called emergent trees, stick up above the rest of the forest. Below these treetops, the crowns of other trees form another layer, the forest canopy. High in the canopy, parrots chatter, doves coo, and orangutans and gibbons swing from branch to branch. Below the canopy, in a layer called the understory, snakes, birds, ants, and other creatures live on tree trunks and in shorter trees. Mouse deer wander and Asian elephants stroll along the lowest layer, the forest floor.

In a mature tropical rain forest, one that has not been logged, the forest floor is shady and easy to walk through. The leaves and branches of the treetops above block sunlight from reaching the forest floor below. So very little grows on the ground. However, along roads, rivers, and in areas that have been logged, the undergrowth can be dense. In those places sunlight reaches the ground. So plants grow thick and tangled, like the "jungle" you often see in Hollywood movies.

WHAT'S DIFFERENT ABOUT ASIAN RAIN FORESTS

Asian tropical rain forests differ somewhat from those elsewhere. For instance, Asian treetops tend to be less interwoven with vines and lianas—woody vines. (However, Asia's forests do contain lianas called rattans, which are harvested for making woven mats and furniture.) When a South American rain forest tree falls, it often pulls down many neighboring trees, which are connected to it by vines. In Asia, where there are fewer vines, fewer trees fall when one tree goes down.

Many Asian forests are dominated by dipterocarps, a family of tremendous trees that stick up, like broccoli heads, above the canopy. Another noticeable feature of Asian forests is the unusually large number of animal species that glide between trees. Flying frogs, flying snakes, flying geckos (a kind of lizard), flying squirrels, and flying opossums have flaps of skin, scales that stick out, and other adaptations that help them glide through the air.

THE WORLD'S MOST AMAZING FLOWER SHOW

In most tropical rain forests, trees bloom, and produce seeds, annually. But each species flowers and drops seeds at a different time of year. In Southeast Asia, something quite different occurs. Once every three to ten years, just after a particularly cool night, dipterocarps form buds and bloom all at once, over large areas of forest. Sometimes almost all the dipterocarps in southern Malaysia bloom at once. Many other kinds of trees bloom at this time, after a cool night, too. Bugs and flies that eat the trees' nectar reproduce rapidly, flying from blossom to blossom. When the flower petals fall, there are so many, you could wade through them, ankle deep!

Weeks later, seeds form, and drop or spin down from the trees, covering the ground with pods and winged seeds. Forest pheasants, green pigeons, squirrels, bearded pigs, and insects dine on the seeds. This bumper crop of seeds, produced only once every few years, is called mast. Masting has advantages for the trees. During a mast, there are so many seeds that the animals cannot eat them all, so more seeds than usual survive and sprout. Oak trees in the eastern United States also mast, producing incredibly large acorn crops every four years or so. The crop is even more than squirrels and jays can eat, so many nuts survive to sprout.

JOIN THE FIG FEAST

Do pigs need figs? In Asian rain forests they do. When dipterocarps are not producing seeds, wild pigs and other animals must find food elsewhere. Many seek out strangler fig trees, which can bloom and produce fruit at any time of year. When figs are ripe, orangutans, gibbons, macaques, flying foxes, squirrels, and hornbills and other birds gather at the fig trees and feast. Asian forests contain hundreds of species of strangler fig trees.

Strangler figs have a peculiar life cycle. When a bird eats a fig, the fig seeds can pass through the bird's body undigested. If that bird flies elsewhere and leaves its droppings on a branch, the fig seeds in the droppings may sprout and grow. They send roots down to the ground and into the soil. The fig plant also grows upward from the branch. Eventually, a strangler fig's roots and shoots can cover the tree where it sprouted. If that tree dies, the strangler fig is often left standing, like a papier-mâché cast of the tree it once covered.

WEARING THIN: THE DIRT ON DIRT

Unlike other forests, tropical rain forests have shallow, nutrient-poor soil, only 1 inch (2.5 centimeters) or so deep. Very few leaves cover the forest floor. Dead plants and animals decompose very quickly, their nutrients used by fungi, plants, and animals. A leaf or a piece of fruit or a dead animal in the canopy may not even fall to the ground. Instead, it may land on a tree branch, and rot there.

As a result of this quick recycling, the nutrients of the tropical rain forest are stored in the trees, vines, and animals—the living forest. (In other forests, many nutrients are stored in the soil, instead.) As a result, when tropical rain forest is cut and removed, what is left behind is poor soil. It is almost impossible for large areas of rain forest to regrow once they have been cut down. Small patches, however, may regrow, if seed sources—from other forests—are nearby.

After rain forest is removed, crops can be grown on the soil for a few years but not much longer. Some farmers burn the slash, the undergrowth left when the trees are removed. The ash from burning fertilizes the soil, improving crops. But after a few years, even with slash-and-burn farming, crops fail. The soil often washes away in heavy rains. Plants die and the soil bakes hard in the tropical sun. What was once a tropical rain forest becomes dry, lifeless land.

BIODIVERSITY

You probably won't want to pick the world's largest flower, *Rafflesia arnoldii*. This rare, reddish-orange blossom weighs 24 pounds (11 kilograms), and stretches 3 feet (almost 1 meter) wide. It also stinks like rotting meat. The smell attracts flies, which pollinate it. But the smell probably keeps florists away!

Rafflesia arnoldii is just one of the many intriguing species that inhabit the tropical rain forests in Borneo. Borneo, the third largest island in the world, is one of many Southeast Asian locales known for high biodiversity. In Borneo alone, scientists have identified 995 tree species growing on 12 acres (4.9 hectares) of rain forest. That's more tree species than grow in the entire continental United States!

Rafflesia *flowers are found only in Borneo's tropical rain forests.*

In the fall of 1997 the skies over Indonesia turned a dingy, yellow gray. The air was so thick with pollution that at times it was hard to see. Ships collided. Cars crashed. A plane went down. Teachers couldn't use blackboards because their students couldn't see them through the smoke. People choked and wheezed. Millions of people went to their doctors for treatment of asthma, lung disease, and other problems caused or worsened by the air pollution. No one knows how many people died as a result of the pollution. But we do know that the smoke came from the burning of tropical rain forests in Indonesia. During August through November, when the fires burned, the haze spread to Malaysia, Singapore, Thailand, and the Philippines.

Why was so much forest, especially in Indonesia, burning in 1997? At first, the Indonesian government blamed the fires on impoverished slash-and-burn farmers, setting fires to clear land. Later, it was revealed that big agricultural companies were largely to blame. They were cutting, clearing, and burning tremendous areas of forest to expand their plantations of rice, oil palm, and other crops.

Some of this type of burning goes on every year. Why was it so bad in this particular year? In 1997, Indonesia was experiencing a drought. The cause of the drought was El Niño, a natural shift in climate that occurs every four to seven years. Because of El Niño, the monsoon rains came later than usual. So the farmer's fires were not put out by the rains as in years past. Plantation owners and farmers also took advantage of the dry weather to burn more forest than usual, and increase the land they could farm.

Fires raged for months. Hundreds of thousands of acres of tropical rain forest were destroyed, including habitat for orangutans and Sumatran tigers. Japan, Britain, Australia, the United States, and other countries sent money, equipment, and firefighters to Indonesia to help put out the fires. But as some blazes were being extinguished, people were still setting others, clearing more land for crops. It was primarily the rains, in November 1997, that doused most of the fires. International environmentalists and health experts are concerned about both the short- and long-term affects of these fires on people and the forest. They are also worried that widespread fires and haze could occur again, unless people work to prevent them.

WALLACE THE WANDERER

In 1854 an English naturalist named Alfred Russel Wallace began an eight-year journey exploring the islands now known as Indonesia. There he discovered something strange. The eastern islands had animals similar to those in Australia. The western islands had more Asian kinds of animals, instead. Wallace concluded that the eastern islands must have once been connected or at least closer to the Australian continent. He believed that the western ones had once been connected to Asia. Wallace's ideas were quite radical for his time, especially because the theory of plate tectonics had not yet been accepted. On maps, geographers often draw "Wallace's line," an imaginary line that shows the division between the islands with Australian types of animals and those with Asian types. Wallace is known for other groundbreaking ideas, too. He came up with the theory of evolution and natural selection at about the same time Charles Darwin did.

DEFORESTATION AND CHANGES IN THE LAND

Centuries ago, Southeast Asia was covered almost entirely by tropical rain forests and monsoon forests. Today, much of this forest has been cut down for lumber, burned for fuel, or cleared for growing crops or grazing animals. Low-lying areas have been filled with rubber tree plantations and rice paddies. People have also farmed hilly, higher ground by building terraces. Terraces, which look like curving stairs, are walled off sections of the hillside. The walled fields keep soil and crops from washing down steep slopes.

Some Asian countries, such as Cambodia, North Korea, South Korea, Indonesia, and Malaysia, have a lot of forest land left. But those remaining forests are being cut quickly, especially in Indonesia. Every minute, a forest area larger than five football fields is cut down in Indonesia. Massive rain forest trees, centuries old, are cut down, shredded, and turned into chopsticks, plywood, toothpicks, and furniture. Much of this material is exported to North America, Europe, Australia, or other parts of Asia. Some tropical woods, such as teak, are particularly beautiful and highly valued for use in making furniture. A big teak log can be worth as much as $20,000, so the incentive to cut the trees is immense.

Despite the destruction, Indonesia still contains some of the largest areas of tropical rain forest outside of South America's Amazon region. Indonesia has preserved about 10 percent of its forest land in parks. But these park areas are not very well policed or protected. So logging, poaching, and burning still endanger them.

SCIENTIFIC SURPRISES IN VIETNAM

When deforestation occurs, people usually cut trees on hillsides last, because they are difficult to reach. In the mountains on the border of Laos and Vietnam, biologists have recently made several startling discoveries. They found three animal species never before identified or studied by scientists. The new species included an antelope-like animal called a saola, and two types of deer. Biologists also rediscovered the Vietnamese warty hog, which had not been seen by scientists for a century. The scientists' first clues that the animals existed were when they saw unfamiliar horns on a hunter's wall. They spotted strange animal skins being sold in local markets, too.

Is New Guinea in Asia? On maps, the island of New Guinea is usually split. The western side, Irian Jaya, is part of the country of Indonesia. So that side is considered part of Asia. But the eastern side, Papua New Guinea, is its own country and is considered a separate entity, not part of a continent. Politically, this division may make sense, but it is odd, considering the island's topography, the contours of its surface features.

In fact, New Guinea has more in common with Australia than Asia. The tremendous island sits on a shallow, underwater extension of the continent of Australia. Thousands of years ago, during an ice age when sea levels were low, Australia and New Guinea were connected by dry land. Australian animals crossed over to New Guinea. Later, sea levels rose, cutting off the connection to Australia. Many of the New Guinea animals then evolved into their own unique forms, different from the Australian ones. Because of its Australian connection, New Guinea has many marsupials—mammals that carry their young in pouches. Wallabies and tree kangaroos on New Guinea may remind you of the ones in Australia. Other amazing New Guinea animals include the world's largest butterfly, the Queen Alexandra's Birdwing butterfly, with a wingspan of 10 inches (25 centimeters). New Guinea's famous birds of paradise have long, showy, colorful tails. Of the 670 bird species found on the island, almost half are found nowhere else on earth.

FACING FACTS AND LOOKING FOR ANSWERS

Some Asian forests that seem intact at first turn out to be almost bare of wildlife. They are eerily silent because there are few birds left to sing. Sun bears, tortoises, turtles, snakes, anteaters, pheasants, and songbirds have been hunted and trapped. These animals are eaten or sold for the pet trade or for use in Chinese medicine. Although many animals are protected by law, in general there are too few people to enforce the laws, and too many needy people who hunt the animals for food and money.

ENVIRONMENTAL EFFORTS

Despite the grim ecological problems in many parts of Southeast Asia, some committed people are finding ways to work to preserve the environment. In 1989 there was a royal decree to ban all logging in Thailand. The ban has helped decrease deforestation in Thailand, although illegal logging is still a problem. But Thailand is now importing logs from nearby countries, increasing deforestation pressure on those countries' forests.

In southern Thailand, villagers recently banded together to protect wild elephants, which are being killed by poachers and farmers. The villagers formed an organization that is working to install electric fences to keep elephants away from crops so people will not harm the animals while defending their crops. They are also planting wild bananas so the elephants will have food to eat.

In Sabah, Borneo, a new foundation is collecting the seeds of tropical rain forest trees and raising seedlings. Foundation workers plant these seedlings in partly logged areas, to help reestablish tropical forests. These kinds of efforts also plant seeds of hope that Southeast Asia's forests and wildlife can be conserved.

CONCLUSION

How many people can an area of land support? What happens when there are too many people, and not enough food to eat and not enough space to live? Some Asian countries are struggling with these questions. In India, park rangers are working hard to keep the growing human population from overrunning national parks. In the Middle East, water shortages are indicating some regions may be reaching or exceeding the number of people the desert biome can support. Meanwhile, the government of Indonesia is paying people to leave the crowded island of Java and move to more sparsely populated islands such as Irian Jaya. But the people already on those other islands are not necessarily glad to see the newcomers arrive, because the immigrants cut down trees and build homes, taking up space and using resources. In significant ways, growing human populations are changing the landscape of the Asian continent.

One out of five people on earth lives in China. Half of the population of the planet lives in the Asian countries of China, India, Indonesia, Russia, Pakistan, Japan, and Bangladesh. But it's not just the sheer number of humans that are changing the Asian landscape, it's the lifestyles they are adopting. Over the last few decades, many Asians have moved from the countryside to big cities. Some are shifting from a rural, farming lifestyle to office work in big cities. As they do so, many begin to desire the products that go along with a "modern" lifestyle: televisions, computers, video cassette recorders (VCRs), washing machines, cell phones, and so on. Manufacturing these items, however, requires natural resources: minerals that must be mined, forests that must be logged, and energy that must be produced. Pollution goes along with these processes. For years Asia has made many of these products for Europeans and North Americans. Now the question is, should they, and can they, and do they want to make these consumer goods for themselves. And what is the cost, in destruction of their own environment and traditional ways of life?

The shift from countryside to city, and the development of new industries, have combined to create something new: megacities. Asia contains some of the world's biggest metropolitan areas: Tokyo-Yokohama, Japan; Osaka-Kobe-Kyoto, Japan; Seoul, South Korea; Bombay, India; Calcutta, India; Manila, the Philippines; Tehran, Iran; and Jakarta, Indonesia. These megacities, cities with more than ten million residents, are crowded and increasingly polluted, particularly as more and more consumers buy cars. Bumper-to-bumper traffic in Jakarta makes any trip a long one. Respiratory disease, caused by air pollution, is a major killer in Calcutta. Some people wear masks to try to reduce the amount of air pollution they inhale.

Solving environmental problems in megacities and other densely populated areas is a big challenge facing Asia. The choices its governments and people make in the next few years will have a lot to do with the quality of life for the children of the continent.

When you walk down a street in Calcutta, India, it's hard to imagine a wilderness. Yet standing on a remote mountain in the Tien Shan, it's hard to even imagine that a city or street or a crowd exists. Asia is a mixture of many varied landscapes and different ways of life: a vast continent of colorful contrasts, environmental challenges, and amazing people.

GLOSSARY

biodiversity—the variety of species of plants and animals in a given area

biome—an area that has a certain kind of climate and a certain kind of community of animals and plants.

climate—a region's long-term weather conditions

cyclone—a storm that rotates about a center of low atmospheric pressure. These storms rotate clockwise in the Southern Hemisphere and counterclockwise in the Northern Hemisphere. This kind of storm is known as a hurricane or typhoon in other parts of the world.

deforestation—the destruction of forest by cutting, burning, or other means

delta—the mud, sand, and other materials deposited at the mouth of a river where the water slows down as it enters a lake or the ocean

desert—a biome that occurs where precipitation is less than 10 inches (25 centimeters) per year

El Niño—the shift in climate and ocean currents that occurs once every four to seven years in the Pacific

endemic—occurring in a specific area, and nowhere else

Indian Subcontinent—the part of India, south of the Himalayas, that juts out into the Indian Ocean. India, Bangladesh, and Pakistan are located on the Indian Subcontinent.

mangrove swamp—a coastal wetland where mangrove trees grow

monsoon—a seasonal reversal of wind direction that brings rain to the Asian mainland

Pangaea—the original landmass that existed 250 million years ago, when the separate continents we know today were all joined together

Panthalassa—the ocean that surrounded Pangaea

plateau—a large, relatively flat area of land raised above surrounding land

poaching—illegal hunting or fishing

polar desert—a cold, dry biome found at the North and South Poles. A similar habitat is found high on mountaintops.

slash-and-burn agriculture—a type of farming in which people cut down the forest trees and burn the slash—the leftover forest debris—in order to clear the land for growing crops

Southeast Asia—a term for countries in the southeast of the continent, usually including Myanmar (Burma), Thailand, Malaysia, Laos, Cambodia, Vietnam, Indonesia, Singapore, and the Philippines

taiga—a biome that is characterized by conifers such as spruce, fir, and tamarack, and occurs north of the temperate deciduous forest

tectonic plate—a large piece of the earth's crust that slides over molten rock below, gradually shifting its position on the earth's surface

topography—the physical contours of a region's surface

tropical rain forest—a forest biome found in the tropics and characterized by warmth, very heavy rainfall, and high species diversity

tundra—a biome found above the tree line. Tundra is characterized by soggy soil in summer, deep permafrost, and low-growing plants. Arctic tundra occurs in the Arctic; alpine tundra is found at high elevations.

Political Map of Asia

INDEPENDENT COUNTRIES LOCATED IN ASIA

NAME	CAPITAL
Afghanistan	Kabul
Armenia	Yerevan
Bahrain	Manama
Bangladesh	Dhaka
Bhutan	Thimphu
Brunei	Bandar Seri Begawan
Cambodia	Phnom Penh
China	Beijing
Cyprus	Nicosia
India	New Delhi
Indonesia	Jakarta
Iran	Teheran
Iraq	Baghdad
Israel	Jerusalem
Japan	Tokyo
Jordan	Amman
Korea, North	P'yongyang
Korea, South	Seoul
Kuwait	Kuwait
Kyrgyzstan	Bishkek
Laos	Vientiane
Lebanon	Beirut
Malaysia	Kuala Lumpur
Maldives	Male
Mongolia	Ulan Bator
Myanmar (Burma)	Yangon
Nepal	Kathmandu
Oman	Muscat
Pakistan	Islamabad
Philippines	Manila
Qatar	Doha
Saudi Arabia	Riyadh
Singapore	Singapore
Sri Lanka	Colombo

NAME	CAPITAL
Syria	Damascus
Taiwan	Taipei
Tajikistan	Dushanbe
Thailand	Bangkok
Turkmenistan	Ashgabat
United Arab Emirates	Abu Dhabi
Uzbekistan	Tashkent
Vietnam	Hanoi
Yemen	Sanaa

COUNTRIES LOCATED ONLY PARTLY IN ASIA

NAME	CAPITAL
Azerbaijan	Baku
Egypt	Cairo
Georgia	Tbilisi
Kazakhstan	Almaty
Russia	Moscow
Turkey	Ankara

DEPENDENCIES IN ASIA

Gaza Strip	under negotiation
Macao	territory of China, administered by Portugal
West Bank	under negotiation

FURTHER READING

(Books for young readers are marked with an asterisk.)

BOOKS

Allen, Tony, and Andrew Warren. *Deserts: The Encroaching Wilderness.* New York: Oxford University Press, 1993.

Arritt, Susan. *The Living Earth Book of Deserts.* Pleasantville, NY: Reader's Digest, 1993.

* Charley, Catherine. *China.* Austin, TX: Raintree Steck-Vaughn, 1995.

* Ganeri, Anita. *The Indian Subcontinent.* New York: Franklin Watts, 1994.

Knystautas, Algirdas. *The Natural History of the USSR.* New York: McGraw-Hill, 1987.

* McClure, Vimala. *Bangladesh: Rivers in a Crowded Land.* Morristown, NJ: Dillon Press, Inc., 1989.

Moffett, Mark W. *The High Frontier: Exploring the Rainforest Canopy.* Cambridge, MA: Harvard University Press, 1993.

Montgomery, Sy. *Spell of the Tiger: The Man-Eaters of the Sundarbans.* Boston: Houghton Mifflin, 1995.

Mountfort, Guy. *Wild India.* Cambridge, MA: MIT Press, 1991.

* Sayre, April Pulley. *Tropical Rain Forest; Taiga; Tundra; River and Stream; Lake and Pond; Wetland.* (Exploring Earth's Biomes series.) Brookfield, CT: Twenty-First Century Books, 1994.

Sinclair, Kevin. *Over China.* Hong Kong: Intercontinental Publishing Corporation, 1988.

Thornton, Ian. *Krakatau: The Destruction and Reassembly of an Island Ecosystem.* Cambridge, MA: Harvard University Press, 1996.

* Withington, William A., Ph.D. *Southeast Asia.* Grand Rapids, MI: Gateway Press, 1988.

SELECTED ARTICLES ABOUT ASIA

NATIONAL GEOGRAPHIC

Archibald, George, "Fading Call of the Siberian Crane," May 1994, 124–136.

Belt, Don, "The World's Great Lake: Russia's Lake Baikal," June 1992, 2–39.

Brashears, David F., "The Siren Song of Everest," September 1997, 63–83.

Carrier, Jim, "Gatekeepers of the Himalayas," December 1992, 70–89.

Cobb, Charles E., "Bangladesh: When the Water Comes," June 1993, 118–134.

Doubilet, David, "The Desert Sea," November 1993, 61–87.

O'Neill, Thomas, "The Mekong: A Haunted River's Season of Peace," February 1993, 2–35.

Schaller, George B., "In a High and Sacred Realm" (Chang Tang and Tibetan Plateau), August 1993, 63–86.

Simons, Lewis M., "Indonesia's Plague of Fire," August 1998, 100–119.

Van Dyke, Jere, "Long Journey of the Brahmaputra," November 1988, 672–710.

Ward, Geoffrey C., "India's Wildlife Dilemma," May 1992, 2–28.

Zich, Arthur, "Before the Flood: China's Three Gorges," September 1997, 4–33.

NATURAL HISTORY

Doubilet, David, "The Desert Sea," November 1996, 48–51.

INDEX

Page numbers in *boldface italics* refer to illustrations.

64